# Model Prayers for Kids

## Volume 1 & 2

Volume 1: For children up to 5 years old

Volume 2: For children over 5 years old

Yesudas Solomon

**WOG BOOKS 114**

*First Edition 2025*

**Author:**

Yesudas Solomon

**Published By:**

Bible Minutes, www.WordOfGod.in




**Download:**

www.WordOfGod.in and www.Archive.org

**Contact Us:**

**WhatsApp:** +91 7676505599
**Email:** wordofgod@wordofgod.in

# Contents

# Notes from the Author

*Greetings of love in the name of Jesus Christ. It is not my intention that this book should be used as a set of memorized prayers. Instead, all the prayers in it are model or sample prayers.*

*Teach them to memorize these prayers at a young age. At the same time, teach them how to take additional prayer points at home, as per your circumstances & situations. Continue to pray in front of children so that your prayers will be an example for them. I would also advice to practice reading the Bible in front of them.*

*Of these 40 prayers, pray five prayers every morning and night: the Prayer of Praise, the Prayer of Thanksgiving, the Prayer of Grace, the Lord's prayer and the Full body prayer.*

*You just need to make them practice for few months, and then they will start doing it regularly.*

*It is our duty to raise our children the way they should be raised. There is no point in not raising them properly and regretting it later. May the Lord Himself give you the wisdom you need and guide you!*

*Yesudas Solomon*

*11 January 2025*

# *Volume 1:*

## *For children up to 5 years old*

## 1. **Prayer of praise**

*Dear God of praise,*

- *Praise to you*
- *Praise to the Father God*
- *Praise to the Son of God, Jesus Christ*
- *Praise to the Holy Spirit God*
- *Praise to the Almighty*
- *Praise to the Holy God*
- *Praise to the Merciful God*

*All praise, honor, and glory be to you, in Jesus' name, Amen.*


## 2. **Prayer of thanksgiving**

*Dear Good Lord,*

- *Thank you for this day*
- *Thank you for being with me*
- *Thank you for your grace*
- *Thank you for your love*
- *Thank you for meeting my needs*
- *Thank you for protecting me*
- *Thank you for blessing me*
- *Thank you for my Dad and Mom*
- *Thank you for my brother / sister*
- *Thank you for grandparents*

*In Jesus' name, Amen.*

*Bible Minutes*

## 3. **Prayer of Grace**

*Dear Gracious God,*

- *Thank you for your grace*
- *Be gracious to us*
- *Give us the grace to live holy*
- *Give us the grace to hear your voice*
- *Give us the grace to be perfect*
- *Fill us with new grace daily*

*In Jesus' name, Amen.*


## 4. **The Lord's Prayer - Matt 6:9-13**

*Our Father in heaven,*

- *Hallowed be your name.*
- *Your kingdom come;*
- *Your will be done on earth as it is in heaven.*
- *Give us today our daily bread.*
- *Forgive us our debts, as we forgive our debtors.*
- *Lead us not into temptation, but deliver us from evil.*
- *For yours is the kingdom, the power, and the glory forever.*

*Amen.*

## 5.  **Full Body Prayer**

*Dear God, make me worthy of heaven.*

- *[Head] - Help me to think only good*
- *[Eyes] - Help me to see only good*
- *[Ears] - Help me to hear only good*
- *[Mouth] - Help me to speak only good*
- *[Hands] - Help me to do only good*
- *[Feet] - Help me to walk in the right way*

*Have mercy on me. Be with me. Bless me. In Jesus' name, Amen.*

## 6.  **Morning Prayer**

*Dear God,*

- *thank you for this day.*
- *Keep me safe,*
- *be with me,*
- *protect me.*

*In Jesus' name, Amen.*

## 7.  **Night prayer**

*Dear God,*

- *thank you for blessing me today.*
- *grant me grace*
- *grant me a good sleep.*
- *Be with me.*

*Bible Minutes*

*In Jesus' name, Amen.*

## 8. Before reading the Bible

- ***Open my eyes*** *that I may behold wondrous things from your law - [Psalm 119:18]*
- ***Open my ears*** *to listen like those who are taught - [Isa 50:4,5]*
- ***Open my heart*** *to observe the things spoken in your law - [Acts 16:14]*

*Amen!*

## 9. After the Bible reading

*Dear God,*

- *thank you for your words.*
- *Give me the grace to obey.*
- *Keep them in my heart.*

*In Jesus' name, Amen.*

## 10. Before eating

*Dear God,*

- *thank you for this meal.*
- *Bless it and*
- *make it nourishing and safe for us.*

*In Jesus' name, Amen.*

## 11. *Before going to school*

*Dear God,*

- *protect me in my journey and in my return.*
- *Protect me from danger and accidents.*
- *Grant me wisdom and memory.*

*In Jesus' name, Amen.*

## 12. *Before studying the lesson*

*Almighty God,*

- *grant me the wisdom to understand.*
- *Grant me strong memory.*
- *Grant me good handwriting.*
- *Be with me.*

*In Jesus' name, Amen.*

## 13. *Before the exam*

*Dear God,*

- *Help me to write well.*
- *Remind me everything that I read and heard.*
- *Be with me.*

*In Jesus' name, Amen.*

## 14. Before going out

*Dear God,*

- *Protect me in my journey and in my return.*
- *Protect me from danger and accidents.*

*In Jesus' name, Amen.*

## 15. After coming home

*Dear God,*

*thank you for bringing me back*

- *safe,*
- *secure, and*
- *healthy.*

*In Jesus' name, Amen.*

## 16. Private Prayer

*Dear God,*

- *thank you for this day.*
- *Bless my studies with wisdom and a good memory.*
- *Be with me,*
- *speak to me, and*
- *shower me with your grace.*

*In Jesus' name, Amen.*

### 17. Family Prayer

*Dear God,*

- *thank you for this day.*
- *Bless my parents, siblings, and grandparents.*
- *Grant us joy, peace, comfort, strength, protection, and grace.*
- *Be with us always.*

*In Jesus' name, Amen.*


### 18. Sunday

*Dear God,*

- *bless this day and my time at church.*
- *Help me sing and worship sincerely.*
- *Be with me and speak to me.*

*In Jesus' name, Amen.*


### 19. Before the worship begins

*Dear God,*

- *thank you for bringing me to church.*
- *Help me to worship, praise, and pray faithfully.*

*In Jesus' name, Amen.*

## 20. After the church worship

*Dear God,*

- thank you for blessing this service.
- Help me to obey your words.

*In Jesus' name, Amen.*

## 21. Sunday school prayer

*Dear God,*

- thank you for bringing me to Sunday School today.
- Help me to worship, praise, and pray sincerely.
- Help me to learn new songs.

*In Jesus' name, Amen.*

## 22. At a relative's house

*Dear God,*

- thank you for this day.
- Bless the elders and children in this house.
- Keep and protect everyone.

*In Jesus' name, Amen.*

## 23. Prayer of Salvation

*(Say the name of the person in the space provided)*

*Dear God,*

- *bless __________ .*
- *Forgive their sins, sanctify and save them.*
- *Prepare them for your heavenly kingdom.*

*In Jesus' name, Amen.*


## 24. Ambulance Prayer

*Dear God,*

- *protect those in the ambulance,*
- *Meet their needs,*
- *Save them,*
- *Prepare them for your heavenly kingdom.*

*In Jesus' name, Amen.*


## 25. Window Prayer

*(Praying for those you see when you look through the window)*

*Dear God,*

- *bless this person.*
- *Forgive their sins,*
- *Save them,*
- *Meet their needs,*
- *Prepare them for your heavenly kingdom.*

*In Jesus' name, Amen.*

## 26. Prayer for enemies

*Dear God,*

- *bless my enemies.*
- *Help me to forgive them.*
- *Save them.*
- *Make them your child.*

*In Jesus' name, Amen.*

## 27. Prayer for Spiritual Growth

*Dear God,*

- *thank you for your blessings.*
- *Forgive my mistakes.*
- *Help me to listen your voice.*
- *Fill me with your grace.*
- *Be with me.*

*In Jesus' name, Amen.*

## 28. Prayer for worldly blessings

*Dear God,*

- *help me to grow in good qualities.*
- *Help me to do good in all I do.*
- *Grant me the grace.*
- *Be with me.*

- Speak to me.

*In Jesus' name, Amen.*


## 29. Birthday

*Dear God,*

- I love you.
- Thank you for this birthday.
- Bless me this year in all I do.
- Grant me wisdom.
- Grant me good memory.
- Be with me.
- Speak to me

*In Jesus' name, Amen.*


## 30. Friend's Birthday

*(Say your friend's name in the space provided)*

*Dear God,*

- thank you for __________.
- Bless __________.
- Forgive their mistakes.
- Bless their parents.
- Save them.
- Prepare them for your heavenly kingdom.

*In Jesus' name, Amen.*

## 31. Prayer for Missionaries

*Dear God,*

- *thank you for the missionaries.*
- *Raise up more missionaries.*
- *Bless them.*
- *meet their needs.*
- *may churches be planted for your glory.*

*In Jesus' name, Amen.*

## 32. New Year Day

*Dear God,*

- *thank you for this new year.*
- *Bless me,*
- *Bless my family,*
- *Bless my friends,*
- *Be with me,*
- *Speak to me.*

*In Jesus' name, Amen.*

## 33. Good Friday

*Dear Jesus,*

- *thank you for your sacrifice on the cross.*
- *I thank you for your victory over death.*

- *Forgive my sins*
- *Save all people*
- *Prepare us for your heavenly kingdom.*

*In your name, Amen.*

## 34. Easter Sunday

*Dear Jesus,*

- *thank you for coming to earth for us,*
- *for dying for our sins,*
- *for rising from the dead.*
- *Thank you for your eternal life.*
- *Save all people and*
- *Prepare them for your heavenly kingdom.*

*In your name, Amen.*

## 35. Christmas Day

*Dear Jesus,*

- *thank you for coming to earth for us.*
- *Thank you for giving us joy.*
- *Save all people.*
- *Prepare them for your heavenly kingdom.*

*In your name, Amen.*

## 36. **Women Day**

*Dear God,*

- *bless all women.*
- *Save them.*
- *Prepare them for your heavenly kingdom.*

*In Jesus' name, Amen.*


## 37. **Mothers Day**

*Dear God,*

- *thank you for my mother.*
- *Bless her and all mothers.*
- *Save them.*
- *Prepare them for your heavenly kingdom.*

*In Jesus' name, Amen.*


## 38. **Fathers Day**

*Dear God,*

- *thank you for my father.*
- *Bless him and all fathers.*
- *Save them.*
- *Prepare them for your heavenly kingdom.*

*In Jesus' name, Amen.*

### 39. Repubic Day

*Dear God,*

- *thank you for India.*
- *Bless all its people.*
- *Save them.*
- *Prepare them for your heavenly kingdom.*

*In Jesus' name, Amen.*


### 40. Independence Day

*Dear God,*

- *thank you for Independence Day.*
- *Bless all people.*
- *Save them.*
- *Prepare them for your heavenly kingdom.*

*In Jesus' name, Amen.*

*19*

# Volume 2:

## For children over 5 years old

*Bible Minutes*

## 1. **Prayer of praise**

*Dear God of praises,*

- *Praise to you*
- *Praise to the Father God*
- *Praise to the Son of God, Jesus Christ*
- *Praise to the Holy Spirit God*
- *Praise to the Triune God*
- *Praise to the Omnipotent God (all-powerful)*
- *Praise to the Omniscient God (all-knowing)*
- *Praise to the Omnipresent God (present everywhere)*
- *Praise to the God of Good*
- *Praise to the Almighty*
- *Praise to the Holy God*
- *Praise to the Seer*
- *Praise to the Preserver*
- *Praise to the Merciful God*

*All praise, honor, and glory be to you, in Jesus' name, Amen.*

**Note:** *Keep adding new prayer points, don't forget.*

## 2. **Prayer of thanksgiving**

*Good Lord,*

- *Thank you for this day*
- *Thank you for being with me*
- *Thank you for your grace*

- *Thank you for your love*
- *Thank you for your word*
- *Thank you for your holy spirit*
- *Thank you for meeting my needs*
- *Thank you for protecting me*
- *Thank you for blessing me*
- *Thank you for good health*
- *Thank you for good studies*
- *Thank you for good teachers*
- *Thank you for keeping me from making mistakes*
- *Thank you for doing good*
- *Thank you for the happiness*
- *Thank you for the peace*
- *Thank you for my Dad and Mom*
- *Thank you for my brother / sister*
- *Thank you for grandparents*

*Amen in Jesus' name.*

**Note:** *Keep adding new prayer points, don't forget.*

## 3. Prayer of Grace

*Dear Gracious God,*

- *Thank you for your grace*
- *Be gracious to us*
- *Mercifully forgive our sins*
- *Give us the grace to live holy*
- *Give us the grace to walk in your ways*

*Bible Minutes*

- *Give us the grace to hear your voice*
- *Give us the grace to know your will*
- *Give us the grace to fulfill your plan*
- *Give us the grace to help the poor*
- *Give us the grace to grow in our spiritual life*
- *Give us the grace to be righteous*
- *Give us the grace to be perfect*
- *Fill us with new grace daily*

*In Jesus' name, Amen.*

**<u>Note:</u>** *Keep adding new prayer points, don't forget.*

## 4. The Lord's Prayer - Matt 6:9-13

*Our Father in heaven,*

- *Hallowed be your name.*
- *Your kingdom come;*
- *Your will be done on earth as it is in heaven.*
- *Give us today our daily bread.*
- *Forgive us our debts, as we forgive our debtors.*
- *Lead us not into temptation, but deliver us from evil.*
- *For yours is the kingdom, the power, and the glory forever.*

*Amen.*

## 5.  **Full Body Prayer**

*Dear God, forgive my sins. Make me holy. Make me worthy of heaven.*

- *Head*
  - *Help me to think only good*
  - *Help me to think what you like*
  - *Help me to remember your words*
  - *Help me to remember the school studies*
  - *Help me to remember advice, suggestions*
- *Eye*
  - *Help me to see only good*
  - *Help me to see what you like*
  - *Help me not to watch TV, mobile*
- *Ear*
  - *Help me to listen only good*
  - *Help me to listen to what you like*
  - *Help me to listen to bible verses*
  - *Help me to listen to your voice*
  - *Help me to listen to mom and dad*
- *Mouth*
  - *Help me to speak only good*
  - *Help me to speak what you like*
  - *Help me not to complain*
  - *Help me to speak kindly*
  - *Help me to read the Bible*
  - *Help me not to forget to pray*
- *Stomach*
  - *Help me not to eat Junk Foods*
  - *Help me not to eat Hotel Foods*
  - *Help me to Eat only good foods*

- Hand
    - Help me to do only good
    - Help me to do what you like
    - Help me to avoid gadgets
- Foot
    - Help me to walk on the right path
    - Help me to walk in your way
    - Help me to walk according to your words
    - Help me to walk according to mom and dad guidance
- Whole body
    - Help me to do your will
    - Help me to carry out your plan
    - Help me to be good
    - Help me to be righteous
    - Help me to be perfect
    - Help me to live holy
    - Help me to give the fruit of the Spirit
    - Help me to become your disciple
    - Help me to live as your child
    - Help me to be ready for your Heavenly kingdom

Have mercy, be with me, bless me, and guide me. In Jesus' name, Amen.

**Note:** Keep adding new prayer points, don't forget.


## 6. Morning Prayer

Dear God, thank you for this day. Keep me safe and guide me to think, speak, and do good. Be with me, help me hear your voice, and empower me to do your will. Grant me new grace, help me grow in the fruit of the Spirit, and equip me with spiritual gifts to bless others. In Jesus' name, Amen.

## 7.  Night prayer

*Dear God, thank you for blessing me today. Forgive my mistakes and grant me the grace to live a holy life. May I remember the good and forget the bad, sleep peacefully, and wake refreshed. Be with me. In Jesus' name, Amen.*

## 8.  Before reading the Bible

- **_Open my eyes_** *that I may see wondrous things from your law - [Ps 119:18]*
- **_Open my ears_** *that I may listen like those who are taught - [Isa 50:4,5]*
- **_Open my heart_** *that I may understand the words of your law - [Acts 16:14]*

*Amen!*

## 9.  After the Bible reading

*Dear God, thank you for your Words. Grant me the grace to obey it, keep it in my heart, and live as a witness to its truth. In Jesus' name, Amen.*

### 10. Before eating

Dear God, thank you for this meal. Bless it and make it nourishing and safe for us. In Jesus' name, Amen.

### 11. Before going to school

Dear God, protect me in my journey and in my return, keeping me safe from danger and accidents. Help me to study diligently, granting me wisdom and a good memory. Guide me to be kind to everyone. May my life be a testament to my faith in you. In Jesus' name, Amen.

### 12. Before studying the lesson

Almighty God, grant me the focus to read carefully, the wisdom to understand, and a strong memory. Guide me to understanding where I lack it and bless me with clear handwriting. Be with me. In Jesus' name, Amen.

### 13. Before the exam

Dear God, help me to write clearly, accurately, and beautifully. Help me to remember what I read and heard and to complete my writing on time. Be with me. In Jesus' name, Amen.

## 14. Before going out

*Dear God, please protect me in my journey and in my return. Protect me from danger and accidents. May I not cause any trouble to others. Help me to go in peace and come in peace. In Jesus' name, Father, I pray, Amen.*

## 15. After coming home

*Dear God, thank you for bringing me back safe, secure, and healthy. In Jesus' name, Amen.*

## 16. Private prayer

*Dear God, thank you for this day. Help me to study well, grow in wisdom and memory, and increase in joy, peace, happiness, and strength. May I diligently read Scripture, learn new songs, and grow in the fruit of the Spirit. Grant me spiritual gifts, that my life may be a witness to my faith. Help me to hear your voice and do your will. Fill me with your grace, and bless me and my home. Thank you for hearing my prayer. In Jesus' name, Amen.*

## 17. Family Prayer

*Dear God, thank you for this day. Bless my parents, siblings, grandparents, and all my relatives. May your voice be heard and your will be done in our life. Grant us joy, peace, comfort, strength, protection, and grace. Help* us to be obedient to my elders and your Word, and to grow in the fruit of the Spirit. Be with us always. In Jesus' name, Amen.

## 18. Sunday

Dear God, as I go to church today, help me to connect with you and with your people. Help me to worship you sincerely, to learn from your Word, and to grow in my faith. Be with me and speak to me as I seek to honor you. In Jesus' name, Amen.

## 19. Before the worship begins

Dear God, thank you for bringing me to church. Help me to worship, praise, and pray sincerely, to listen attentively to your Word, and to understand and remember what I learn. Speak to my heart. In Jesus' name, Amen.

## 20. After the church worship

Dear God, thank you for blessing this service. Help me to obey the words I have heard and to never forget what you have spoken to me. Be with me and guide me. In Jesus' name, Amen.

## 21. **Sunday school prayer**

*Dear God, thank you for bringing us to Sunday School today. Help us to worship, praise, and pray sincerely, to listen attentively to your Word, and to learn new songs. May we all grow in wisdom, in the Word, and in the fruit of the Spirit, walking in a way that pleases you. In Jesus' name, Amen.*

## 22. At a relative's house

*Dear God, thank you for this day and for the opportunity to be with our relatives. Bless the elders and the children in this house, and bless all they do. Keep them safe and grant them joy, peace, comfort, strength, protection, and grace. Meet their needs, save them, and sanctify them, preparing them for your heavenly kingdom. In Jesus' name, Amen.*

## 23. **Prayer of salvation**

*(Say the name of the person in the space provided)*

*Dear God, bless _________. Forgive their sins, sanctify and save them. Show them your grace, favor, and mercy. Protect them, be with them always, and fill them with the fruit of the Spirit. Make them your disciples and prepare them for your heavenly kingdom. In Jesus' name, Amen.*

## 24. Ambulance Prayer

*Dear God, protect those in the ambulance and meet their needs. Forgive their sins, save them, and sanctify them, preparing them for your heavenly kingdom. Grant all people courage to help others, and fill them with love and mercy. Protect me and my family from similar situations. In Jesus' name, Amen.*

## 25. Window prayer

*(Praying for those you see when you look through the window)*

*Dear God, bless this person. Forgive their sins, sanctify them, and save them, making them your child. Meet their needs and fill them with joy, peace, comfort, and strength. Guide them to your church and prepare them for your heavenly kingdom, along with their family. In Jesus' name, Amen.*

## 26. Prayer for enemies

*Dear God, bless my enemies with joy, peace, comfort, strength, wisdom, and good character. Save them and make them your children, preparing them for your heavenly kingdom. Take away any hatred I have for them and help me to love them as you love them. In Jesus' name, Amen.*

## 27. Prayer for spiritual growth

*Dear God, thank you for your blessings. Forgive my sins and mistakes and help me to live a holy life. Guide me as I read Scripture, sing praises, and listen for your voice, that I may do your will and obey your Word and my elders. Help me to grow in the fruit of the Spirit, be anointed by the Holy Spirit, and use my spiritual gifts to be a witness to my faith. Be with me. In Jesus' name, Amen.*

## 28. Prayer for worldly blessings

*Dear God, help me to help the poor, grow in good qualities, and do good in all my thoughts and actions. Grant me the grace to forgive, show mercy, and be kind to everyone. Increase my wisdom, knowledge, and understanding, especially in my studies, that I may understand and remember my lessons. Guide me to do your will, walk obediently, and live as a witness to my faith. Be with me. In Jesus' name, Amen.*

## 29. Birthday

*Dear God, I love you. Thank you for this birthday. Bless me this year in all I do, granting me new graces, wisdom, and a good memory. Help me to honor my parents and live a life pleasing to you. Keep me holy, be with me, and guide me to do your will. Grant me joy, peace, comfort, strength, and the grace to live as your disciple, sharing your love with others and being a witness to your truth. In Jesus' name, Amen.*

## 30. Friend's Birthday

*(Say your friend's name in the space provided)*

*Dear God, thank you for _________. Bless _________. Forgive their mistakes and help them to live a holy life. Grant them wisdom and success in their studies. Bless their parents and help them to be a positive example to others. Fill them with joy, peace, happiness, and strength. Save them, make them your child, and prepare them for your heavenly kingdom. In Jesus' name, Amen.*

## 31. Prayer for Missionaries

*Dear God, thank you for the missionaries. Raise up more missionaries for the harvest field. Bless them, meet their needs, and equip them with spiritual gifts and graces. May many come to salvation, and may churches be planted for your glory. In Jesus' name, Amen.*

## 32. New Year Day

*Dear God, thank you for this new year and for new blessings. Bless me, my family, my church, my friends, and all people. Grant us joy, peace, comfort, strength, and the grace to be your disciples, sharing your love and being witnesses to your truth. Save us and prepare us for your heavenly kingdom. Be with me. In Jesus' name, Amen.*

## 33. Good Friday

*Dear Jesus, thank you for dying on the cross for my sins, breaking the curse, and giving me victory. Forgive my sins, cleanse me with your blood, and make me righteous. Be with me and guide me. Grant me the grace to live as your disciple, sharing your love and being a witness to your truth. Save all people and prepare them for your heavenly kingdom. In your name, Amen.*

## 34. Easter Sunday

*Dear Jesus, thank you for coming to earth for us, for dying for our sins, and for rising from the dead. Thank you for your eternal life. Grant me the grace to be your disciple, sharing your love and being a witness to your truth. Save all people and prepare them for your heavenly kingdom. In your name, Amen.*

## 35. Christmas Day

*Dear Jesus, thank you for coming to earth for us, bringing us joy, peace, forgiveness, and salvation. Grant me the grace to live as your disciple, sharing your love and witnessing to your truth. Save all people and prepare them for your heavenly kingdom. In your name, Amen.*

### 36. Women Day

Dear God, bless all women with joy, peace, comfort, and strength. Save them and prepare them for your heavenly kingdom. In Jesus' name, Amen.

### 37. Mothers Day

Dear God, thank you for my mother. Bless her and all mothers. Grant them many years, joy, peace, health, and strength. Save them and prepare them for your heavenly kingdom. Help them to walk without difficulty and to be obedient to your will. In Jesus' name, Amen.

### 38. Fathers Day

Dear God, thank you for my father. Bless him and all fathers. Grant them many years, joy, peace, health, and strength. Save them and prepare them for your heavenly kingdom. Help them to walk without difficulty and to be obedient to your will. In Jesus' name, Amen.

### 39. Repubic Day

Dear God, thank you for India and its laws. May good laws prevail and unjust laws be changed, that justice and fairness may reign throughout the land. Bless all its people with joy, peace, comfort, and strength. Save them and prepare them for your heavenly kingdom. In Jesus' name, Amen.

## 40. Independence Day

*Dear God, thank you for Independence Day. May everyone be free from sin, curses, harmful addictions, and all forms of bondage including TV, mobile phones and gadgets. Bless all people with joy, peace, comfort, and strength. Save them and prepare them for your heavenly kingdom. In Jesus' name, Amen.*

## **<u>Our other books (Printed / E-Books)</u>**

1.  ஒரு வருட வேத வாசிப்பு திட்டம்
2.  One Year Bible Reading Plan
3.  சங்கீதமும் நீதிமொழிகளும்
4.  சங்கீத புத்தகத்திலுள்ள ஜெபங்கள்
5.  தமிழ் - வேதாகம மனப்பாட வசனங்கள் பாகம் 1
6.  தமிழ் - வேதாகம மனப்பாட வசனங்கள் பாகம் 2
7.  Tanglish - Vedaagama Manappaada Vasanagal Bagam 1
8.  Tanglish - Vedaagama Manappaada Vasanagal Bagam 2
9.  Bible Memory Verses Volume 1
10. Bible Memory Verses Volume 2
11. Bible Coloring Books 01 Creation [Tamil, English]
12. Bible Coloring Books 02 Adam and Eve [Tamil, English]
13. Bible Coloring Books 03 Cain and Abel [Tamil, English]
14. Bible Coloring Books 04 Noah [Tamil, English]
15. ஞாயிறு பள்ளி பாடங்கள் - தொடக்கநிலை - பாகம் 1
16. Tanglish - Gnayiru Palli Paadangal - Thodakkanilai - Baagam 1
17. Bible Coloring Book for Sunday School Syllabus Beginners - Volume 1
18. வேதாகம தியானங்கள் பாகம் 1 40 லெந்து நாட்கள் [ஆசிரியர். கிளாடிஸ் சுகந்தி ஹாசிலிட்]
19. வேதாகம தியானங்கள் பாகம் 2 40 லெந்து நாட்கள் [ஆசிரியர். கிளாடிஸ் சுகந்தி ஹாசிலிட்]
20. வேதாகம தியானங்கள் பாகம் 3 - [25 கிறிஸ்மஸ் தியானங்கள். ஆசிரியர். கிளாடிஸ் சுகந்தி ஹாசிலிட்]
21. வேதாகம தியானங்கள் பாகம் 4 [365 நாட்கள். ஆசிரியர். கிளாடிஸ் சுகந்தி ஹாசிலிட்]

22. தம்பிரான் வணக்கம் 1578 [ஆசிரியர்: பழங்காசு சீனிவாசன், ஏசுதாஸ் சாலொமோன்]

23. தமிழ் பைபிள் 1714 பாகம் 1 (மத்தேயு முதல் அப்போஸ்தலருடைய நடபடிகள் வரை)

24. தமிழ் பைபிள் 1714 பாகம் 2 (ரோமர் முதல் வெளிப்படுத்தல் வரை)

25. ஒருவருட வேதாகமம் (தமிழ், English, Telugu, Kannada, Malayalam, Hindi)

26. ஒருவருட வேதாகமம் - சம்பவங்கள் நடந்த கால வரிசைப்படி (தமிழ், English, Telugu, Kannada, Malayalam, Hindi)

27. தமிழ் வேதாகம ஒத்தவாக்கிய விளக்கவுரை

28. அபிஷேகம் [ஆசிரியர்: Rev. Dr. A. பிரகாசம்]

29. என் வாழ்வில் தேவனுடைய கிருபை [ஆசிரியர்: Rev. Dr. A. பிரகாசம்]

30. தமிழ் இணைநிலை வேதாகமங்கள்

31. English Parallel Bibles

32. கர்த்தருக்குச் சித்தம் [ஆசிரியர்: Rev. Dr. A. பிரகாசம்]

33. சீகன்பால்குவின் ஓலைச்சுவடி பிரசங்கங்கள்

34. தமிழ் வேதாகம பழைய மொழிபெயர்ப்புகள்